To Miles Lewis Miller,
welcome to the wild world
D. E.

Thanks and love to my family
and naturalists everywhere
R. D.

Text copyright © 2020 by David Elliott
Illustrations copyright © 2020 by Rob Dunlavey

First edition 2020

Library of Congress Catalog Card Number pending
ISBN 978-0-7636-9783-9

19 20 21 22 23 24 TLF 10 9 8 7 6 5 4 3 2 1

Printed in Dongguan, Guangdong, China

This book was typeset in Caecilia.
The illustrations were done in watercolor and
mixed media with digital rendering.

Candlewick Press
99 Dover Street
Somerville, Massachusetts 02144

visit us at www.candlewick.com

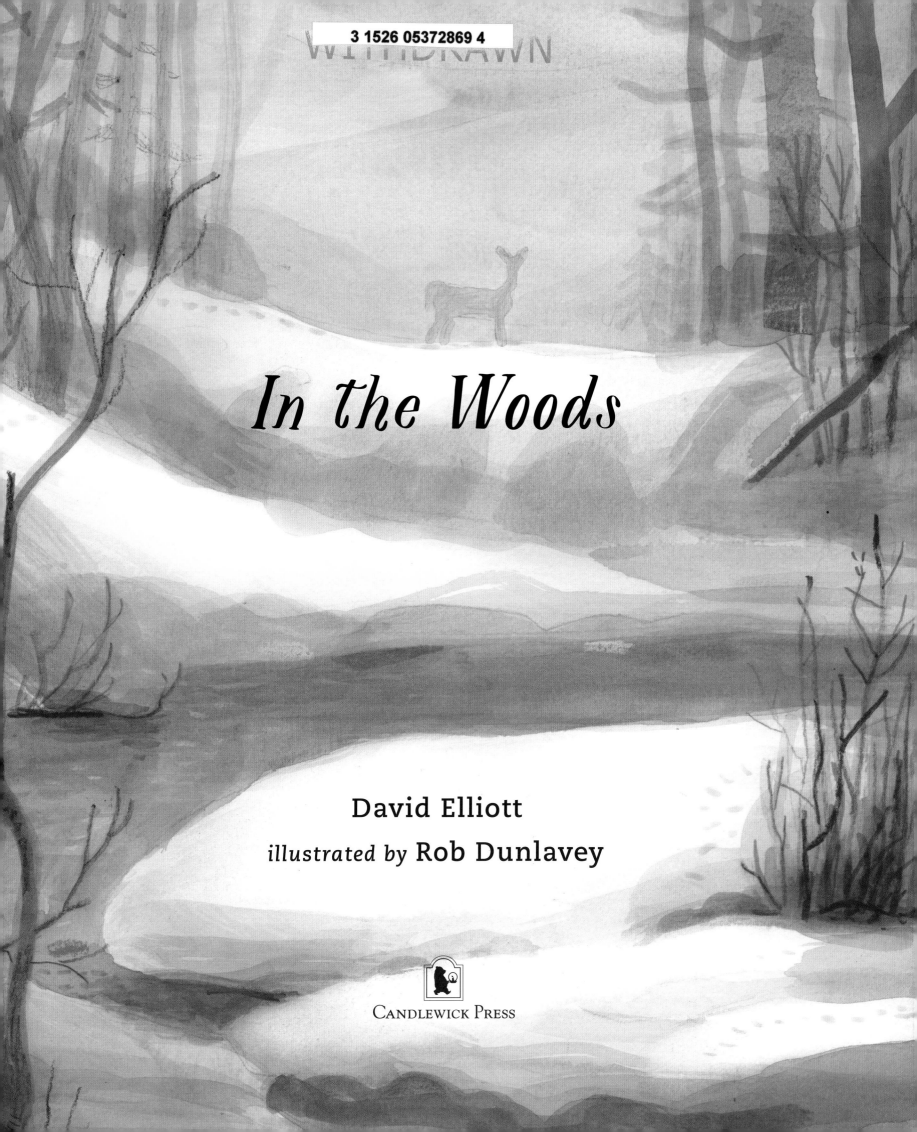

In the Woods

David Elliott

illustrated by **Rob Dunlavey**

CANDLEWICK PRESS

The BEAR

The shadow stirs
in its musky den.
A yawn,
a stretch,
a muffled snort,
and then
the shadow emerges
breathing in the snowmelt air.
What voice has whispered
to its sovereign heart:
Awake!
Awake, oh, sleeping bear!

The FOX

Stands red
against the April snow,
a fiery prophecy
of things to come.
She is thinking of her kits;
they must be fed.
A dreadful thought
for some.

The SCARLET TANAGER

Look! There!
A flash of red
in the spring
green of the trees,
as if the forest air
is branded,
burned.
It's spring!
Huzzah!
The cowslip is blooming;
the scarlet
tanager has returned.

The OPOSSUM

Your rattish snout, your naked tail
dragging on the woodland trail:
you're not a classic beauty.

You bump along the woodland track,
your babies clinging to your back:

there's beauty, too, in duty.

The SKUNK

Give the skunk
a lot of
room, unless
you care for
strong perfume.

The PORCUPINE

Does not hurry.
Never scampers.
Will not scurry.

Beware this surface nonchalance;
when rushed, she gives
a barbed response.

The FISHER CAT

Does not like fish.
Is not a cat.
I don't know what
to make of that.

But when you are
as fierce as she,
there's no need for
consistency.

The HORNET

Avoid you at all cost
is the prevailing sentiment.
But how unoccupied the
woods, without your buzz-
ing tene-
ment.

The MILLIPEDE

You are   a detri
tivore,   a word
I'd nev   er heard
before.   It means
you dine   on last
year's   leaves
fallen   on the
forest   floor.

The MOOSE

Ungainly,

mainly.

The BEAVER

Jack-of-all-trades—
    that's the beaver
Some might say
    he's an overachiever.
Architect
    and engineer,
family man
    and arborist.
Musician, too!
    When danger's near,
he's a jazzed
    percussionist.

The WILD TURKEY

Is a lesson in the language arts;
so much to learn from him:
with his waddle and his wattle,
he's a walking homonym.

The BOBCAT

Those tufted ears, the amber eyes,
that ambushed second of surprise
　　　when the bobcat leaps!
The silent spring, the empty space,
and all the world is spotted grace
　　　when the bobcat leaps!

The RACCOON

The Powhatan

call you *aroughcun,*

"the one who scratches

with its hands."

But the eyes behind

the mask reveal

"the one who understands."

The DEER

Enters the clearing like a dancer
from behind a curtain.
Only when he's certain it's safe
do the others appear.
A troupe of dancers now—the deer.
But somewhere behind, a breaking branch—
and buck and doe and fawn
                    are gone.
How silently they go—the deer.
Nothing left but
heart-shaped tracks.

These, too, will disappear.

Notes About the Animals

THE BEAR
Guess what? Some scientists think that bears don't actually hibernate! True hibernators, such as ground squirrels, must wake up once a week or so to eat and pass their waste. But bears can go for about three and a half months without eating or moving their bowels. Also, unlike true hibernators, bears wake very quickly from their long winter's nap. Many scientists now refer to the bear's denning habit as "winter lethargy."

THE FOX
Foxes have such a developed sense of hearing that they can hear voles and other animals tunneling underground. Sometimes the prey that a mother fox brings back to her kits is still alive. This gives her kits an opportunity to hone their hunting skills before they must fend for themselves. A female fox is called a vixen. The male is called a dog.

THE SCARLET TANAGER
These spectacular birds are famous for being hard to spot, as they love to be high up in the forest canopy. Keep your eye out for them in early spring, when they've returned from their winter homes in South America but the leaves of deciduous trees are not yet fully out.

THE OPOSSUM
The opossum is North America's only marsupial—in other words, the continent's only mammal with a pouch. Opossums can have up to twenty babies in a single litter. Once they are developed enough to crawl out of the pouch, baby opossums hitch a ride on their mother's back.

THE SKUNK
Skunks have very poor eyesight, which is why cars are such a danger to them and why we see so many of them by the side of the road. Generally, a skunk produces enough scent for five or six healthy sprays. Once the scent is depleted, it takes about ten days to produce the next batch.

THE PORCUPINE
North American porcupines can have up to thirty thousand quills. Contrary to popular belief, porcupines cannot shoot their quills, but they do come off quite easily, a fact to which many curious dogs can attest. The word *porcupine* comes from the Latin for "quill pig."

THE FISHER
Fishers, sometimes called fisher cats, are members of the weasel family and have a reputation for being especially ferocious. That reputation may be well deserved, considering that the fisher is the only North American animal that dines on porcupines.

THE HORNET
The bald-faced hornet is the one that most of us recognize as a hornet. But it's actually a kind of wasp. In fact, *all* hornets are wasps (though not all wasps are hornets). Most hornets are a little fatter than other wasps. They're also more aggressive and will sting without any provocation. Unlike honeybees, hornets can sting repeatedly.

THE MILLIPEDE
The word *millipede* means "one thousand feet," which is a little bit of a fib, since individual millipedes usually have only two hundred legs. (They're born with just three pairs.) There are big differences between millipedes and centipedes. Both have segmented bodies, but a centipede has only one pair of legs per segment, whereas a millipede has two. Another difference? Millipedes are harmless, but some centipedes have a venomous bite.

THE MOOSE
Moose are the largest members of the deer family. Bulls shed their antlers, or paddles, every fall and grow new ones in the spring. The larger the paddles, the older the moose. A full-grown set can weigh as much as forty pounds. A moose's worst enemies are not bears or wolves, but tiny brain parasites and ticks, both of which have contributed to a decline in the moose population in North America.

THE BEAVER
After the capybara, the beaver is the largest member of the rodent family. Like the teeth of all rodents, a beaver's teeth are constantly growing. Beavers use theirs to gnaw on wood for food and fell trees for lodge-building. Slow on land, beavers are strong swimmers and can stay underwater for up to fifteen minutes.

THE WILD TURKEY
Normally, we don't think of turkeys the way we might think of other birds, that is, in the sky. But wild turkeys are agile fliers in spite of their size and can fly for up to a quarter of a mile. If you happen to be in the woods at night, look up. You might see a flock of these birds roosting in the treetops. Benjamin Franklin wanted the wild turkey to be America's national symbol instead of the bald eagle.

THE BOBCAT
Nocturnal hunters, bobcats are ambush predators, which means they stalk their prey, bide their time, and then at just the right moment leap on their victims and deliver a deadly bite. Bobcats can bring down prey double their size and can leap up to ten feet/three meters.

THE RACCOON
What do raccoons have in common with pigs? The male is called a boar, the female a sow. In captivity, a raccoon can live for as long as twenty years, but in the wild that number is greatly reduced, usually to only two or three. Diseases and cars are a wild raccoon's worst enemies.

THE DEER
Baby deer, called fawns, are born with no scent, which is why the mothers protect their young by having very little contact. Fearful that their scent may draw a predator, mother deer visit their newborns only to feed them. When a deer is alarmed, it raises its tail like a flag and wags it to warn its companions.